novum ➤ pocket

AF273138

Marie Thérèse Kiriaky

Escaping Forward

novum pocket

© 2023 novum publishing

ISBN 978-3-903382-92-3
Cover photo:
Goran Šafarek | Dreamstime.com
Cover design, layout & typesetting:
novum publishing

www.novum-publishing.co.uk

DEDICATED TO

Blessed are those who mourn,
for they will be comforted.

And to every modest Syrian,
who tolerated unbearable struggles ...
"The world has forgotten you,
but you stayed in our hearts."

Regards,

CONTENTS

Out of My Body

In huge numbers, men, women, and children gather in the square near the camp, waiting for the relief-aid car. It is loaded with food rations to be distributed to the refugees, and I am one of them. The weather is hot, and the crowding is at its worst, organizers are asking us to line up quietly. I put my child on the ground, next to a wall that blocks the sun and protects him from the scrambling of people. I was in distress and could barely breathe anymore; my chest felt tight from those haunting looks I kept getting.

I wonder where I've seen these looks before, the ones that are obvious even in darkness, the ones coming from the unknown, from far, far away, from a swaying tunnel, meandering just like the body of a black snake writhing and wiping everything around it. Oh, yes, now I remember. I got these looks throughout many stages of my life. These looks keep chasing me and burning me with their fire as if hands were touching every curve of my body. These looks attempted to take off my clothes, aiming to reveal what was hidden, penetrating my body to reach my bones.

I also got these looks when puberty hit me, when turning into a lady was obvious, with my body getting curvy and beauty blooming in it. These looks were reflected in men's eyes living in our quarter. These looks penetrated through my clothes, searching for the blossoms hidden underneath. And then, I noticed these looks in our family men's eyes and their not-so-innocent touches while they pretended to "play" with me. Again, these same looks were reflected in the eyes of my classmates at university; and again, with my colleagues at work. Until my life became a daily struggle, from the moment I woke up and left home in the early morning, to the looks I got from neighbors, bus drivers and their passengers, and everyone I encountered at work.

Such looks overflow with desire ... with lust ... with all that's forbidden. Such looks are scary, they almost burn the person they fall upon. Such looks always make me feel like they drain my humanity and dignity. Such looks cancel out my soul and focus only on my body ... transforming me into an object, with no soul.

The looks of these eyes got closer and closer, and I felt the heat of the body carrying them. I couldn't touch the body, but I smelled his sex-interlocked scent. A few seconds later, he touched me; my neck, face, and body curves until he reached sensitive parts of it. The only thing left was for the train to enter the station. All this happened while we stood in line, waiting for aid allocated for refugees.

All my attempts to keep the man away from me failed. What made things worse was my inability to fidget, resent, or even utter a sound, since my voice could lead to a crime. At that time, everyone would feel dignified and make their case. However, most of those present would also wish they were in the shoes of that hungry-eyed man; from the bottom of their hearts. In addition, everyone already felt tense and there was no room for more tension, especially with the fact that every mistake costs a life. In other words, the situation easily portrayed our local Syrian saying, 'Even after dying, there's still a struggle finding a grave' ... [1]

Oh, God, I'm tired ... And I can do nothing about it ... The long-awaited relief-aid car doesn't come every day. My children are starving and are eagerly waiting my return. They are dreaming of the food I'll get them. We have been eating bread and drinking tea for over a month. Even the herbs I used to pick from the outdoors ran out. My kids are very thin, their stomachs are bigger, and their eyes are bulging.

As for my husband, who was hit by a landmine; he's sitting in the corner of the tent, this tent that we barely got after paying the last of all we owned. He lost both legs, and his wounds are still aching. However, he has patience. He bites on his hands when an episode of pain comes; a kind of pain that is unbearable. My soul goes out to him, and my little heart can no longer take it.

My husband's suffering and pain did not intercede for me in front of these looks ... Men passing these looks started verbally going too far and sometimes even trapping me in some corner.

They asked how I'm doing. How could I bear the bad situation I'm in, with my wounded husband, who is not able to carry out his marital and financial burdens?

---

1 'Even after dying, there's still a struggle finding a grave': It's a Syrian proverb meaning the situation is difficult or that the person saying it is suffering.

Men chasing me outside the tent didn't stop there. Rather, they still followed me into the tent itself. They used to visit us, pretending to check up on my husband, while they dared to peek at me with their gluttonous and impudent eyes. They claim friendship with the poor man and show their sympathy for the crisis he's going through, and they sit for long hours chattering. Meanwhile, I am forbidden from getting comfortable in the tent, which is barely four square meters.

As despair almost seeped into my heart, the relief-aid car finally arrived. The relief-aid workers began distributing the aid bags. The crowding got worse, and so did the distance between my body and that of the stranger. I couldn't leave the line and I couldn't ask for help either, for help to get rid of this clinging creature sticking to me and touching every part of my lower body, from my back to my feet.

I felt like throwing up and I tried my best to bear the situation I was in, all because I couldn't return to the tent empty-handed. If I did, I wouldn't be able to handle my childrens' disappointment, agony, and deprivation of a warm meal after long months of leftovers.

After great effort and a long time, I finally got my food ration. I took it and took off running. I called my little child, the youngest, who was waiting for me near the line, just where I left him. He ran and hugged me tightly. I took him and went to our tent as if it were our last refuge.

I've always wondered what else I could do to protect my body, dignity, and pride!

Hijab[2]! I wore that.

Jilbab[3]! I wore that too.

Makeup! I no longer wear it.

Perfume! I no longer wear it either.

I haven't checked myself out in a mirror in a long while, yet I still have these looks hovering around me. Is it possible for these looks to only see my body? But how come when my whole body, head-to-toe, is covered in fabrics hiding all its curves?

I still have many questions running through my mind, and I could not find an answer to any of them. Don't those passing such looks have mothers, sisters, wives, relatives, or even friends? And if they do, would they accept them being humiliated the way I was and I still am?

Would they accept men preying on the need of women for the most basic right, which is the right to live with dignity ... or do such behaviors portray the part of our culture that sees a woman as an object, that anyone can own and control its destiny!

I pledged to not be beaten by those eyes invading my life day and night. I will not accept this reality being imposed on my family and me. I am determined to confront the owners of these eyes and push them to the point where they are forced to apologize.

---

2 Hijab: is a veil worn by many Muslim women in the presence of any male outside of their immediate family. It usually covers the head and chest, and sometimes the face.

3 Jilbab: refers to any long and loose-fit coat or outer garment worn by some Muslim women.

I put my child on the only bed we own and light the fire under a bowl of water, preparing to wash my body and clothes in an attempt to wash away the disgusting smell, the smell that got me dizzy. I started rubbing my body like crazy as if I wanted to purify it. If it were up to me, I would have loved to get out of it, with no hesitation.

DEANSHIP PARTY

I was going through Al-Nazeel, a local newspaper, 'in a dead corner' – as they would say in Damascus – of our quiet neighborhood. My teacher gave it to me, asking for my opinion.

I wasn't the only student who got a copy of this newspaper, my friends got them too. This newspaper wasn't just any newspaper, for it represented the voice of a banned party in Syria. Therefore, we had to make sure that no saboteur saw us reading it since the intelligence agencies had eyes planted all over the country eavesdropping on the citizens. They considered that every legitimate citizen needed to be accused, of either treason, spying, or dependence on hostile parties. You could find these saboteurs wherever you went. You might even find them in your wardrobe, under your pillow, or even in your bathroom. There was no place where they could not stalk.

That night determined my fate, as well as that of my friends. In the blink of an eye, our lives had been changed. We got out of one place and time and went straight into a similar purgatory, which was just between heaven and hell.

They dragged us like sheep, with our heads down, hands and feet cuffed, into the horrific Tadmor Prison. Tadmor Prison could make some people panic the second they heard its name. In Tadmor, we realized that we had come to a place where there was no return to our normal lives.

Feeling embarrassed, we entered the jail. We were greeted immediately with beats, punches, and insults while heading to the assembly hall; and they came from the guards lined up on both sides of the hallway leading to the assembly hall. We tried protecting our heads; however, our handcuffed hands prevented that. As a result, some of us got serious injuries and bruises, while the rest almost lost their eyes.

We stood in lines. The guards brought four chairs, as well as four barbers circulating among the prisoners. They started shaving our heads. With the fall of each strand of our hair, a piece of our dignity dropped to the floor.

They took our clothes and all we had. We were twenty-five guys from the same school, and some of us were from the same family and some from the same neighborhood. We were distributed among the prison cells; more like we were crammed into prison cells with others ... we were barely able to breathe. That night, we had no dinner, since we had arrived late. There was no room for us to sleep on our backs or stomachs. Therefore, we slept on our sides as the chief of our cell shouted at the top of his lungs: "Sword." That meant "sleep," like the edge of a sword, on your side. The cells looked more like sardine cans.

Ten days passed. We ate three leeches daily, every morning, noon, and night. On the eleventh day, our group was taken to the courtroom. We entered the room; it smelled like rottenness. In the center of the room sat a man, whom we knew was the judge, with two other judges by his side.

The prosecution attorney read our names out loud and asked us to stand up when we heard our names. Everyone was trembling and scared of the next ... The harsh judge's voice filled the room as he said, "Did you know you're accused of belonging to a banned party in the country? and that everyone belonging to this party is subject to the death penalty?"

A deadly silence took over the room, and the judge chanted loudly: Execution according to Article 5130. Some of us tried to respond or refute the idea, but we were told to remain silent.

The judge continued. According to him and on what was proven. "We, judges of Tadmor Prison, sentence first the accused, Muhammad Ali, to 20 years in prison with hard labor instead of the death penalty, given that he is a minor."

As for the rest of the defendants in the hall, whose names were previously read, they were sentenced to death by hanging until they were dead, and the sentence would be enforced the next morning in the prison yard. He banged his gavel on the table, announcing the end of the trial.

Dying with the rest was much easier on me than being the only one alive among my friends. Dying with them was mercy. Oh, God, what is this test that you have put me in? Just because of my young age, I was sentenced to prison instead of hanging. It was like I had betrayed my friends to a place I didn't know!

Everyone broke down. Everyone started screaming, crying, and protesting. Everyone was in disbelief. Is it reasonable to pass a sentence in a single moment to execute twenty-four young men? without them even being given a chance to defend themselves or protest against it! Where is the justice? and what had we done to deserve this sentence? Is reading a banned newspaper enough to justify such judgment?

We went back to our cell, sadness hovering around us. That night, none of the prisoners could sleep. We all agreed that the ones who were to be executed should state their names out loud so that the rest of the prisoners could memorize the names and inform their families of their deaths ... since the prison administration did not give the detainees' families any information about the fate of their sons in prison.

Morning arrived, and we all gathered in the yard. Tears were streaming down several faces. And the process of execution began. Voices rolled in as loud as they could ... Ihab Omar, Yasir Muhammad, Ahmed Al-Laithi ...

After two and a half hours, the death party came to an end. We returned to the prison cells. I was transferred to a different cell with some other detainees ... My fever grew high. I fell into a state of delirium. I was bedridden for more than ten days with no medication and little food. My colleagues took care of me and tried their best to help me to recover. The closest of them was Ghassan, who was five years older than me.

Ghassan was a cheerful and friendly person. He was able to bring joy to everyone around him and turn all painful events into funny scenes ... In short, he was a source of joy and strength for us all. He also motivated us to continue our bitter lives.

Ghassan and I remained inseparable for a long time, which enabled me to discover many things about him and vice versa ... about our studies, our family, the things we loved, and the things we had in common. We often spent long hours discussing various issues that concerned us.

One day, a guard came and asked Ghassan to get ready since he was invited to the "hangman deanship party". He had recently joined the prison staff.

A "deanship party" ... I didn't get that! I asked my old pals in the prison about its meaning. One of my fellows, Abu Muhamad, answered, saying, "My son, 'deanship party' is a torture session that cuts the guard's strings with all that is humane. When a new guard joins the prison, the ritual preparations for him to become a murderer begin. The ritual goes through various stages and takes several days. In the first two days, a guard is forced to watch the torture of prisoners to learn about the various methods and types of torture they used."

During the next two days, the trainee is given a whip with which he strikes the prisoners. It is a tank cable consisting of iron wire surrounded by strings, it is as thick as the width of a hand. It can even injure its holder if he does not learn how to use it. For example, one wrong move could cause the holder to lose his ear. Therefore, the guard learns the methods of striking using this cable, by waving it in front of him, left and right, up and down ... until he can use it correctly. In the last two days of the deanship, the jailer beats a prisoner to death. Then he is declared to have become a dean and is celebrated for joining the Killers Club.

Sadness overwhelmed everyone. Men cried as they bid farewell to Ghassan, who continued smiling as usual. However, during that time he became absent-minded. When he approached and embraced me, I collapsed. I was unable to stand. He helped me up, put something in my hand, and whispered in my ear. "In case I don't return, which is most likely to happen, I hope that you will hand over my cross to my mother and she will figure it out by herself that I am dead."

My Cross? I didn't know Ghassan was a Christian! All I knew was that he had escaped military service several times and was punished more than once until he ended up in the terrible Tadmor Prison. I had thought that it was for Muslims only.

Ghassan was taken and the torture session began. We heard his voice and screams; some of us were even able to see him through the cell's tiny window ... long hours, louder cries. The cries shook our being. With every blow, his dream was being scattered on the walls of the cell and our souls were scattered with it. We prayed for God to take his soul quickly to ease his pain.

Ghassan collapsed. The executioner thought he'd fainted and tried to wake him up by kicking and beating him. However, Ghassan did not move. The executioner threw a pail of water over his face, but still, there was no movement. The executioner shuddered and called his boss, who came quickly and put his hand on Ghassan's neck feeling for his pulse.

Shaking his head, the responsible officer said, "The prisoner is dead." He then turned to the executioner and told him. "If you do that again, I will shave your head. Pay attention."

The incident had a huge impact on us, and it was just too much for me to handle. My friend passed away, taking my smile with him. I stayed in that state of purgatory for seventeen years, until I was released with a general amnesty just three years before the end of my 20-year term in prison.

On the Border

Thanking God for their safe arrival in Turkey and for crossing the borders safely, Hanan and her four daughters knelt on the ground and kissed it. Finally, after a journey that had lasted for more than a month, during which they had seen all kinds of horrors and suffered great hardships, Hanan stood and embraced her daughters. They cried their hearts out until they calmed.

Hanan, a lawyer from the city of Homs, had resisted the urge to leave for more than three and a half years. She clung onto the land, for she was not a person who would accept surrender easily. Despite what she had been through with her family, she remained determined to stay in her homeland. She did not want to become a refugee or a displaced person. She believed that when one left one's homeland, one's value was reduced. But she was forced to leave, for her and her daughters to survive.

Who would have expected what happened in Homs, a city that used to be a shining example of the accomplishment of the coexistence of its inhabitants? They were divided into three-thirds, Sunni, Alawite, and Christian. That all vanished with the disaster that befell Syria and tore its social strings apart. Hatred floated to its surface, and everyone played the game of mobilizing individual sects … and a system based on the theory of 'divide and rule' came into being.

In Homs, the people who were divided into many religious and sectarian components, young adults, men and women, began to practice peaceful protests. The protests soon turned into something more like celebrations, and the people involved launched new songs, banners, and slogans every week, which proclaimed the freedom and the unity of the Syrian people. The slogans were translated into multiple languages. The protests had turned into something that looked like wedding celebrations.

The security officers couldn't believe what was happening, they tried curbing the revelers with all the power and weapons they had. They even tried to fill the city's central square with shattered glass so to prevent the protestors from revolting there. They then began to besiege certain neighborhoods by preventing them from accessing food and medicines, and they banned all citizens from entering or leaving their neighborhoods.

Hanan lived in one of the neighborhoods, and the security forces began raiding homes. They searched for young men and drove them to detention campuses and prisons. Among those arrested were Hanan's brother, cousins, and husband. Every detainee spent long months in underground basements.

After almost dying from torture and starvation, her husband was released. Later, her cousins were also released. However, her brother remained under arrest and his fate was unknown for several months.

One day, the bad news came out that her brother had died and Hanan was asked to go and receive her dead brother's body. Her husband wanted to accompany her, but she refused to allow that. She was worried about what could happen to him, especially since his health wasn't good. She also feared that he would be arrested once again.

Hanan went to the security branch on her own. She was admitted to a large hall full of corpses, a scene that caused her to panic as she had to look into everyone's faces to identify her brother's body. All the faces and bodies were swollen and bluish. She found him and recognized him with difficulty, thanks to the mole on his cheek.

Hanan and the Sheikh prepared the body for burial. They carried the corpse and buried it after the Sheikh had read the necessary passages very quickly. The Sheikh feared he'd also be arrested, for the security officers asked him to quickly finish reading the prayers. How hard was that! Only two people were there to bury her brother, who used to fill the world with his vitality and love of life. He did not deserve to be buried this way, as if he were a criminal whose family wanted to get rid of him. His family and loved ones were not able to read al-Fatiha for his soul. All these rituals were done quickly and silently.

Hanan returned home unable to move. She stayed in bed for two days. When she got up, she demanded that her daughters should commit to staying at home and should not participate in any protests. The family's loss was great but would be even greater if one of the girls was arrested.

Unfortunately, the loss of her brother was not the only loss, as it was followed by the martyrdom of her cousins, and her husband was arrested once again. Hanan tried to ask about him at the security branch offices, but she was prevented from entering and threatened with arrest. Nine months later, she was summoned by security officers to receive the body of her dead husband. She arrived at the office, and after searching and checking, an official asked her to look at a computer to confirm that a picture was that of her husband. It was indeed a picture of her husband.

Hanan asked for the body to be released to her and the official said, "There is no corpse, we buried it." Hanan panicked and asked how she could be sure that he had died. The official replied, "Is our word not enough, or do you doubt what we say? Do you want to come, too, and visit us?" Hanan was afraid and concerned about her four daughters; so she pulled herself together and returned home defeated.

The strange thing is that the more oppressive the regime in power gets, the more the youth increases its uprising; until the day came when the security forces arrested all the girls and women of the youth who had joined the ranks of the revolutionaries. They were driven like a herd to the central square and were raped in full view of their families, and then simply killed in cold blood.

That was then Hanan decided to flee with her daughters. She claimed illness and obtained a report from a friend of hers saying that she needed an immediate heart operation, and that way, she managed to leave the besieged neighborhood and went to the hospital in Damascus. From there, she returned to the coast and then went to the mountains which formed the border with Turkey, and she then eventually arrived in Tibet after a long journey.

NASMA

"Oh my God, what a beauty!" The investigator said as he went around Nasma's thin body, which was trembling with fear. He watched her jade-bead-like green eyes wandering around the place, trying to explore it.

Nasma was a 20-year-old girl from Aleppo. She was arrested while she was trying to sell her paintings in the Sabeel Public Park. She was now in a security vault. It was dark, except for the light shining in the middle of the room. A musty smell mixed with blood and sweat filled the room.

The investigator's voice rang out, commanding the recruiter. "Take off her Hijab … let's see what's hidden underneath!" The recruiter did not understand what the officer wanted. He gawked into his eyes, so the officer yelled again. "I told you to take off her Hijab!"

The recruiter extended his trembling hands and took Nasma's veil off, after her desperate attempt to prevent him from doing so. Powerless, she was handcuffed. Her black wavy hair dropped and covered her back down to her waist.

The investigator blew a long, blistering whistle and told her. "What a great loss it is that such beauty works with terrorists! Before lending them a hand, didn't you think about what could happen to you, if you were to get arrested?"

The girl answered in a terrified voice. "What terrorists? I don't know any terrorists, I swear."

"Oh, and you also have the nerve to lie?" The investigator shouted and then continued. "By the way, do not open your mouth before I ask you to." He tapped her forehead with his finger. "Got it?"

Nasma couldn't utter a word, for words got stuck in her throat, as it went dry. So, she shook her head with tears streaming down her face.

The officer asked, "What were you doing in the park?"

"I was trying to sell my paintings," she replied.

"Selling your paintings? For the sake of whom?"

"To help the poor."

"The poor, you say? Or is it the terrorists?"

"Believe me, I was doing it for the poor!"

"As long as you don't cooperate with us, the investigation will take too long." Then, the investigator asked, "Were you the link between the terrorists? From whom was the information?"

Nasma answered. "Trust me, Mr. Investigator, I just wanted to help the poor in our area who have no breadwinners."

"Well, you said it yourself ... 'those who have no breadwinners' ... that is, those whose breadwinners went to fight against the state ... In other words, those who joined the terrorists!"

"No. No. That's not what I meant."

"Have you noticed that you're getting on my nerves? I'll repeat the question, who were you cooperating with?"

"I swear by God Almighty; I don't get what you're saying."

"No. Seems like talking will get us nowhere with you," the officer said angrily.

The investigator called on the recruiter and ordered him to whip her feet. Nasma cried and tried to plead with him, so he decided to help the recruiter to tie her. The beating began at the bottom of her legs.

He said, "I will go with fifty strikes for now. Let's see if that beautiful mouth of yours utters all you have to tell us."

Then the strikes began. Two. Three. Four. Twenty. Twenty-eight. Nasma stopped counting, for she had fainted. She only woke up after the recruiter emptied a pail of water onto her.

The officer ordered the recruiter to sit Nasma on the chair. Nasma opened her eyes and stared at the officer as if seeing him for the first time. She was utterly surprised as he was eating with great appetite a fully grilled chicken making strange sounds, expressing his appreciation for its taste.

The officer stared back at her and said. "You haven't eaten since yesterday, of course. How about a piece of chicken breast? No. No. Chicken thighs are much better." He offered her a piece of meat and asked her to take it. Hesitating to take it, Nasma stretched out her hand. Before she touched it, the investigator screamed and turned the table onto the floor.

"What do you think you're doing? You wanna eat?" He pulled her up by her hair and threw her onto the floor. "Bitch. Food is only for the deserving."

He started kicking and punching her until she fainted once again.

Nasma woke up to find herself in a cramped cell with about forty other women. They all gathered around her. Trying to relieve and comfort her, they put their hands every-where she had been whipped. The eldest among them, trying to calm her down, said. "Be patient, my daughter … God is with you. This nightmare must come to an end."

The ladies started introducing themselves. Widad, Razan, Samira, Amal, Nada, Mary, Nouhad. Razan gave her a piece of bread; Maysa prepared her a cup of tea and Haifa wiped her wounds. It all seemed to her like a sacred ritual that women used to practice. It's a ritual in which each of them knows her role. It was a ritual in which her female colleagues walked around as if they were priest-esses in the Temple of Bel. They rotated around Nasma and read out some incantations. The eldest woman wiped her hair while holding her in her arms.

One of them said. "O Allah, I ask you by every name you have that allows you to respond to my prayer, I ask you in the name of every right who has rights with you, and I ask you in the name of every right you have upon everyone who is below you to protect Nasma, support her and relieve her pain."

The rest replied. "Amen."

While the other said. "Virgin, most holy, Mother of the Word Incarnate, Treasurer of graces, and refuge of sinners, I fly atop your motherly affection with lively faith, and I beg of you the grace ever to do the will of God. Into your most holy hands, I commit the keeping of her heart, asking you for the health of the soul and body, in the certain hope that you, my most loving Mother, will hear my prayer."

Rapid footsteps began approaching the door of the cell. Terror took over the room. The women held each other's hands as they waited to discover who would be asked for.

29

The door swung open and the guard shouted. "Nasma!"

Nasma clung to her fellow inmates. The guard did not wait for her to move and immediately pulled her out. He dragged her along the ground, for she could not stand on her swollen feet, and led her to the investigator's room.

The investigator stared at her and said. "I'm sorry this has happened to you. I know you're in pain, but as you know it all depends on how you respond to me. The more you reveal the truth, the sooner the moment of your release will come."

Reveal. The word of revelation got stuck in her head. She had once heard it from her lover in an intimate moment. He used it as he stated that the highest level of love is a revelation.

The investigator said. "Let's start all over again, who were you cooperating with?"

Nasma said nothing for she was lost in her thoughts.

The investigator slammed his hand on the table and shouted in Nasma's face. "Haven't you heard me? I'll repeat my question once more, what cell were you cooperating with? What role do you play in it?"

Nasma desperately said. "Trust me, Mr. Investigator, I have no idea what you're talking about!"

One slap, just one slap came across her cheek and knocked her to the ground as the investigator yelled. "Don't make this harder on the two of us. Speak!"

Nasma collapsed and burst into tears. The investigator screamed. "Do you know what you'll be exposed to? Let me explain the matter to you. We will start, for example, with ghosting[4], then with electrifying. We'd then go with nails being pulled, burnt with cigarettes on your body, and the most beautiful of all, rape? What do you think?"

Nasma collapsed and fell at his feet, begging for mercy, as well as her family's against the indignity.

He said. "You get to choose where we'd kick off." A few minutes later, he added. "I think it's a pity if we distort this beauty. I think we should enjoy it. What do you think? Are you ready to talk?" ... Nasma cried and swore that she would not lie.

The investigator went crazy and called on Nizar. Nizar entered, looking like three people combined, with great height and great width. He was like a monster in the shape of a human being.

The investigator told him. "Take your time, Nizar, since our inmate did not cooperate with us."

Nasma shrank like a bird in the room's corner. Her screams rose as she saw this monster approaching her, slowly, slowly as he began to loosen his belt.

The investigator left the room. Amid the sound of Nasma's pleading and wailing, her voice reached her cellmates. An hour, two, or three. Time stopped for Nasma. Until she reached the stage of feeling as if she had been

---

4 Ghosting: The infamous al Shabeh (Ghost) torture method is common in the Syrian Regime's detention centers, in which the detainee's hands are tied behind her/his back, then she/he is raised by the same rope, which is tied to the ceiling, leaving her/his body suspended from the ground so the full weight is hanging from the wrists.

separated from her tiny body; she was no longer able to think. Her thoughts went to her home, to her mother's lap, her siblings, and her father's tender voice.

They took her back to the dungeon like a dead body. The women of the temple cried for her and performed the usual rituals. They washed her young body and wiped the effects of the invasion. Days and months went by, during which Nasma was exposed to many different kinds of torture.

Finally, they made sure that she had hidden nothing from them. Her pardon was issued.

Nasma bid farewell to her cellmates, who had become her friends, and walked past the gates until she reached the door of the large prison. The closer the distance between her and her family, the more her heart beat. She was not sure whether this was from fear or longing

Many questions ran through her head ... Who would she meet first once she got out? Would she be able to answer their questions? Would she be able to describe what she had endured during her detention? A thousand questions and great concerns clouded her joy at meeting her family.

The gate was opened, and Nasma went out with hesitant steps ... The daylight blinded her. It took her a few minutes to adjust her eyesight to her surroundings, as well as to discern her father's face. Nasma hurried toward him. She saw his sad face, in which the wrinkles had deepened. Gray hair had invaded his head and left no black spots on it. His back had become more arched because of his careworn life. He welcomed her, saying. "Hello, thank God for your safety." He did not allow her to embrace him and walked in rapid steps, after asking her to follow him by beckoning her to follow.

She followed his steps quickly to the bus station. She was stumbling as if she was just learning to walk. Nasma was in a great state of fear and anticipation of what awaited her in the coming days.

She got onto the bus and sat across from her father, who avoided looking at her, while she also avoided looking at him.

Her mother greeted and kissed her, a little coldly, however, and so did all of her brothers and sisters. The house seemed strange … sad … dull. The curtains had been replaced by other darker-colored curtains and the windows were closed. Even her family's clothing was black.

A whole hour went in silence. It felt like forever. Her dad broke the silence saying. "The trouble we got in and the shame that befell our name is much greater than a person can bear on his own. However, we'll all join hands to face this shame, the society, and its people … until God Almighty is kind enough to us to make those around us forget the misfortunes that befell us." He then continued. "So don't expect things to return to what they were before you entered the detention. Moreover, the freedom you used to enjoy, going in and out whenever you feel like it, has come to an end. From now on, you get to leave the house only with one of your brothers after asking for permission. As for going back to study, this is also over. There is no room for painting either in this house anymore. The only thing that you can do is help with the house chores and cooking. One more important thing, more like an order. I don't wish you to show up in front of the house's guests and our neighbors. Likewise, it is better not to appear in front of me as well, as long as I'm home."

He gave her some harsh looks, lacking every sort of emotion, and said. "I hope I do not have to repeat my words. I also hope that you have understood what I mean; there is no room for mistakes, only one mistake exposes you to a punishment that you could never imagine. Now you can go back to your room."

Her tears were not cascading down her face, for she was utterly shocked. Nasma tried opening her mouth to object, but she stopped after a signal from his hand and a stern look in his eyes. She stood up and dragged herself away. As she withdrew, she tried to look into her mom's eyes, as well as her siblings, but everyone just looked away. However, her older brother was an exception, for his gaze showed anger and hatred. She couldn't understand why though.

She sat crying at the edge of her bed, her father's words ringing in her ears. She felt bad for herself. How could it be possible that he had not asked her how she was doing? Neither he nor anyone else in the family had asked. Was it possible that she meant nothing to them now? She was waiting for them to ask a simple question like; how had she managed to get through the days she spent in prison. That was the least they could do if they didn't want to hear about the psychological and physical pain she had gone through. All that mattered to them was saving the family's honor and reputation, as well as erasing what had happened to her from the people's memory. Where had all this cruelty come from?

She then remembered the words of her friends in prison … 'She must be patient … She must give her family some time to accept her among them again'. However, her friends didn't mention that she would not find a warm hug that would restore the reassurance and security that she had lost. Not only that but there was another feeling that she did not understand which was the strange look in the eyes of those around her.

Every night, while she had been in prison, Nasma had dreamed of compassion and love, which would ease her pain and sadness upon her return to her home. Not only that, but she was also expecting help from them to forget the harsh days that she went through because she only intended to remember the goodness of her work. Perhaps she was expecting too much. Perhaps she was supposed to be more aware of feeling the pain of those around her. However, she felt depressed about being treated as the perpetrator, not the abused.

Nasma woke up one day to the sound of her mother approaching her, only for her mother to find her sleeping under the bed on the floor. Her mother couldn't understand why, but Nasma wasn't able to explain her fears, which were caused by the fact that she had become so used to sleeping on the floor for long months in the darkness. Now, although her room was comfortable and bright compared to her cell, that brightness prevented her from sleeping.

Her mom asked her to get ready to help her around the house, since everyone had already gone to their work or school, except for her older sister who was getting ready to go to university. Nasma tried to say something, but her mother didn't give her the chance to do so as she mentioned the huge amount of work that needed to be done.

Nasma got ready and started to work, which she later thanked God for because it kept her mind busy instead of her negative thoughts and sorrows. As soon as she finished cleaning the house, she entered the kitchen to help her mother. All day long, she worked with her mother without starting any conversation. They simply made small talk related to the work. That continued until evening drew in and everyone started returning home.

Nasma helped her mom as they prepared the dinner table. She put the right number of plates on the table for her family members. As her mom came to check on the table, she angrily removed the extra plate. Nasma had put a plate and chair at the table for herself. Her mother then asked her to remove the extra chair.

When Nasma looked at her mother with her inquiring eyes. Her mother looked away and said. "Have you forgotten what your dad said? He doesn't want to see you when he's home. It's better for you to return to your room ... Eat there. You must thank God that your dad still allowed you to return home and live among us once again."

Nasma was shocked. She couldn't believe her ears. Her tears fell and she returned to her room. She remembered once again what her cellmates had said about patience.

The same thing happened for several more days, during which Nasma was unable to talk to any of her family, except her mother. Her isolation became worse.

One day, her older brother wanted his mom to iron one of his shirts. So, her mother asked Nasma to do that, but the brother went crazy about it. He yelled at his mom. "Didn't I tell you that I don't want her anywhere near me? and that I don't want her to touch my stuff or defile me? She must be grateful I haven't killed her yet."

Nasma ran off to her room, feeling very scared and insulted, and locked herself in her room. She didn't go out until the following day, only to perform the same duties and burdens placed on her.

One morning while she was dusting the carpets on the balcony, she saw her childhood friend and neighbor Maysa on the balcony of her house and greeted her. Maysa replied shyly and in a low voice. Suddenly Maysa's mother came and started screaming at her daughter. She told her to get into their house. "Did I not tell you not to talk to her? Did I not warn you? Did I not tell you that she's a shame? Do you want to be like her?" Etcetera ...

Nasma entered the living room and closed the door. She was distraught, with pain in her heart. The word 'shame' revolved in her head and a big question 'Why?' Was she the one who chose to enter the prison? Was she responsible for allowing them to use violence against her? Had she allowed them to rape her? Did no one understand the pain she was feeling?

Why did they not treat her like any man who had just gotten out of prison? What was the difference between her, and any man who had spent time in jail? – when many such men had also been exposed to what she had been exposed to, including rape?

Days and nights passed. Loneliness filled her life. Oh, how she dreamed of a hand that would pat her shoulder and helps her to go on with her life. Oh how much she dreamed of someone who would ask her how she was feeling and what had happened to her. Oh, how she dreamed of someone helping her heal the wounds she suffered from, the wounds in her soul ... that pure and innocent soul of hers. She kept asking herself what sin she had committed. She became even more and more isolated in her room. She became like a ghost, wandering around the house with no one seeing her.

On a day off, everyone is at home. On such days, Nasma usually stayed in her room, unless her mother needed her to finish some chores. As noon came and after everyone had had lunch, they all went back to their rooms to rest and take their nap. Nasma's mother came to call Nasma to clean the kitchen. She tried to open the door of her room, but she wasn't able to do so. She knocked and called her. There was no answer. Her mother was surprised and knocked again. There was no answer. She hurriedly called her husband, who came angrily to help her open the door. He threatened Nasma, but she did not open the door.

The family gathered in front of the door, so Nasma's father asked her brother to break the door down. The door hung open and everyone entered the room. Nasma was hanging from the ceiling fan. Everyone was silent. The shock was very obvious on her father's and her siblings' faces. However, the mother collapsed and fell to the ground, crying for her daughter.

They found a letter written by her on the bed. The father took it and asked his older daughter to read it because he wasn't wearing his eyeglasses. The daughter took it and began to read it:

> "My beloved mother,
> My beloved father,
> My beloved brothers and sisters,

I know that what I'm going to do is forbidden in several religions, for no one has the right to take the soul but its Creator.

But my soul is imprisoned in this body, and I yearn to liberate it. By the time you'll find my message, I'll have liberated it and freed my soul from this life.

I'm now in a world where there is no room for pain and shame. No one will ever be able to harm me ever again.

I have relieved you from my distress and from the looks others gave you. You can now live in peace. The shame that befell the family has been wiped out. You can walk in the street with your heads held high. I tell you that a culture that sacrifices its children for the sake of customs and traditions that hinder our lives is miserable. It leaves us no space for hope. But, my loved ones, many questions are still stuck in my head. I hope you'll have time to answer them, even if within yourselves.

What does the word father mean? Does it not mean safety?

What does the word mother mean? Does it not mean love?

What does the word sibling mean? Does it not mean a bond?

Have you asked yourselves ... how did you differ from that executioner who insulted me?

Wasn't it right for you to console me and stand by my side, help me overcome my crisis, and take back my rights from those who violated my dignity?

Did you ask yourselves, "Is this how she was supposed to be rewarded because she thought of others? because she tried to alleviate the suffering of the poor?

My beloved ones, I leave your world for you, not feeling sorry. Despite everything, you are still in my heart ... and I forgive you.

Nasma."

Escaping Forward

The cell's door hung open and a pile of meat was pushed in. It had no features, neither its neck nor waist could be distinguished. It was an enlarged body crammed into baggy clothes that had receded in several places to reveal the skin of the body, whose color was a mélange of yellow, blue, brown, and red.

This pile of meat belonged to a hump-wrapped woman who entered the cell walking slowly, because of her heavy weight. Her hair was fluffy and long locks covered her face. She was swaying left and right while making terrifying sounds that gave the impression that the owner of these voices was imbalanced and had features of madness. Whenever someone touched her, her screams and wails filled the room.

No one was able to come close to her, because, in addition to her panic over everything revolving around her, she smelled awful (the least we could say). Her smell combined filth and blood, it was just disgusting. She hasn't showered for a long time and her hands hadn't touched water for a very long time.

She hallucinated, making incomprehensible noises. She hummed different verses of multiple songs. She didn't calm down once for the whole day. She paced around the cell dozens of times. She also hit her head against the wall dozens of times. That went on all day long ... until she made everyone tired.

Some women tried to calm her, but she didn't respond to them. Things continued that way until she got on the nerves of some women. They started beating her, hoping that she'd become quiet. However, that only made her insanity and her screaming worse.

I, along with some other women could not take it any more. Therefore, we pulled her away; pulled her over to the corner of the cell, gave her a cup of water, wiped her hair and hands, and patted her shoulders. She somehow calmed down. A cellmate asked her what was her name, and she replied. "Janet." She continued shaking her body like some readers shake when they study the Bible. One of us came forward and started chanting a church hymn to calm her down.

"Under thy protection, we seek refuge, Holy Mary,
despite not our petitions in our needs,
O pride of the innocents,
O sea of gifts running in this world,
O the door of heaven, O mother of sacrifice
O eye of hope, O light of guidance."

Janet woke up the next day, terrified by the jailer's voice as he told us to get up and start our daily work. It included cleaning, arranging, cooking, etc. but the first thing that came to our minds was taking Janet to the bathroom. It took four of us women to take off her clothes and force her to sit on the toilet seat.

Cleaning her took more than an hour. As for her hair, no attempts in cleaning or combing it worked, so we went with cutting it. Those hours were difficult. Finally, we were able to get her into a clean loose-fitting nightgown and we went back to the cell along with her. She was so happy. As the poet says:

"Who has ever seen like my love? She's like a full moon.

She walks in the room today, but her hips never follow soon."[5]

We gave her a bed close to mine since she liked me, and she never let go of my hand ... I stayed near her until she fell asleep. She slept for about ten hours straight, and then woke up for dinner. I grabbed a plate for her and fed her myself. She looked at me and it felt strange. Her eyes didn't shine with gratitude, but with intelligence ... as if she wanted to tell me something I couldn't seem to catch.

A week later, Janet started getting better. Her screams subsided, as well as her movements. On the eighth day, we were all asked to go out to the prison's yard. Everyone, with no exceptions. We stood in lines waiting for the head of the prison, who had called us together to inform us of his new orders. He showed up, all creepy and serious, with his bodyguards surrounding him.

He said. "Tomorrow, we're expecting a visit from a delegation from the International Red Cross. They want to see you and your situation in prison. All of you are required

---

5 The poet uses such words to describe his beloved, who's fat. He means by "She enters the room today but her hips never follow soon" that is because she's fat, and her hips come into sight a while later.

not to speak with any of the members of the delegation and you will refuse that when requested. If any of you is asked whether there are female political prisoners, the answer will have to be a 'no'." He then continued. "Of course, upon the delegation's entry, you have to show the extent of your love for our country and our beloved president by carrying his pictures and the country's flag. It's also preferable to chant slogans in support or to sing a patriotic song. You have the ultimate freedom of choice. Now for the good news, we'll be distributing new clothes for everyone. You have to wear them tomorrow to appear decent in front of our guests. I hope that you'll be responsible enough, we don't want foreigners to get the wrong idea about our country and its policies." He turned his back and left the yard, announcing the end of the meeting.

Clothes, pictures, and flags were distributed that same day. The prisoners started cleaning their cells and preparing themselves. They took turns to the bathroom for whatever preparations they needed to make. Janet seemed happy with what was going on around her, just like a child on Christmas eve.

The next day came. Before the delegation attended, the jailer came and called Janet's and my names, saying. "Everyone stays here except for Janet, who will be taken somewhere else, and Safaa, who has to accompany her, as she is the only one who can calm her down."

Janet went back to her hysterical state and madness, prompting the jailer to forcibly drag her into a forgotten underground room. He ordered me to silence her or else I would be punished.

We went into the room, and he locked the door. Janet and I stayed together, facing each other. I turned to her only to see she was calm and balanced. She stopped screaming, wailing, and moving. Everything was back to normal. Astonished, I asked her if she was okay.

"Yes," she said, but later added, "you're shocked, aren't you?"

I replied. "I'm actually in disbelief. I'm wondering why all this has happened?"

She replied in a calm voice. "The only way I could escape from the hell of the security centers and the bitterness of the torments I was subjected to, from which I would die in the end, just like many cellmates of mine did – was to be crazy."

A Wreath of Throne

Today, I'll talk to you in my beloved language ... Arabic! ... and not in my mother tongue. I'll convey to you the love that my heart overflows with toward all of my brothers in humanity. I will not be a war devil. I will not be a false witness to the injustice, oppression, and systematic brutality my Syrian brothers and sisters are facing.

Nor will I be detached from my teachers, the symbol of truth, the sun of justice, and the Redeemer and the Savior. Thirty years of my life have been spent on Calvary Road. Thirty years of love filled my heart. But this love slipped right through my fingers and was taken by the winds of evil.

On the day I arrived at her port, she acquired my sentiments. We became acquainted with each other. She became me and I became her. I saw my face in hers. I no longer knew who I was and who she was. It was as if I saw myself in the mirror. My soul flowed on her soil like albumen water, transparent, in her love.

The attractive Qalamoun Mountains fascinated me. I found my soul in Deir Mar Musa al-Habashi, located at the desert gate. Here my dream began to kick off. It was a Sufism-Christian-Muslim joint project. I've always believed that the monk or nun was part of the society in which they lived and that they had to be effective in dealing with it. So, I started working in the public sphere ... in an area where the harmony between earth and heaven, between earth and man, existed.

The restoration of the monastery took me many years of my life, for I repaired it with my hand piece by piece, stone by stone. I didn't forget the other monastery, which is about half an hour away from the Monastery of Mar Musa al-Habashi, nor the caves surrounding it, in addition to the library, visitors' rooms, and the park for spiritual sports. People started to visit it for prayer, meditation, and inter-religious dialogue. It was and still is my absolute belief that every person can reach God and his word through every path he sees.

As Ibn'Arabi said, "Creatures held beliefs in God, and I believed all they believed."

I also believed in everything that a man believes in, as Ibn Arabi also said.

"My heart can take on any form: a meadow for gazelles, a cloister for monks,

For the idols, sacred ground, Ka'ba for the circling pilgrim, the tables of the Torah, and the scrolls of the Quran.

My creed is love; Wherever its caravan turns along the way, which is my belief, my faith."

The day has come when we will experience all that we believed in, in terms of freedom and dignity for the human being. It was also time to test all we believed in from the interfaith dialogue that took me thirty years of contemplation, dialogue, and debate, as well as from writing about this topic. I knew that the road to freedom was full of obstacles, it wasn't easy in this country. I repeatedly tried to find an outlet to break the wall of closure pursued by the authority, fearing for its position, and sending out many messages to the head of the authority. I attempted to create bridges between the people of power and our people, who are thirsting for every right a human being needs to live decently. Unfortunately, I did not succeed.

My voice got higher and higher and the security authorities could no longer bear it. My peaceful activities disturbed them, so I was arrested and interrogated. Later, I was forced to leave my homeland Syria. I was the one who dreamed of carrying the Syrian nationality. I wanted my life to end in it and I wanted to be buried in it. I have recommended this, provided that my last resting place is in the monk's cemetery, under an olive tree.

The call of love made me join the ranks of the opposition, making my primary national goal the Islamic-Christian reconciliation. That way I applied what I believed and wrote in my book 'Faith in Jesus and love of Islam'.

Before saying goodbye to my country and my family, I wrote this letter to my loved ones, hoping that I would come back soon.

"Goodbye, my family in Al-Qalamoun

At the time I leave the country heading to a painful exile – God only knows that I would have preferred to have been buried on this beloved land's soil with the martyrs of freedom or even have been arrested in some jail – my heart is comforted by sending a message of thanks to the dear people of Qalamoun through free pages addressing our free youth. I apologize to the competent authorities for not requesting in advance the security approval and permission to print. One of the six points of the Annan plan is the recognition of my right to exercise freedom of opinion and expression, although for this reason I am being expelled.

Thirty years of companionship, cooperation, good neighborliness, and some difficulties as well have passed. I've tried this ancient civilizational root that shows loyalty to one's religion, as well as respect and appreciation for the neighbor's religion. Nevertheless, among the rich wheat ears, I could see with concern that poisonous and thorny herbs were growing. Those were almost curbing the community culturally, religiously, and institutionally. The environmental reserve closed, lectures and dialogue seminars were banned, and work was suspended in all its dimensions. However, the spirit was not suppressed.

In March 2011, as the sprouts of the Syrian spring blossomed, my residency ended. Ever since then, I haven't been able to travel outside the country to meet my elderly parents.

In the past months, I had to put aside caution and fear, because I saw in the horizons the outbreak of civil war, thousands of deaths, and the distortion of our homeland's beauty, they are our honorable young women and men. I tried, and still am, to preempt the practice of mature democracy. Perhaps it will overcome tyranny with the weapon of truth, not bullets.

Now, goodbye Qalamoun and its dear people. In my heart, I've got images of kind faces, pure hospitality, and cruel minds that only walk with conviction.

Goodbye to my relatives, Christians, and Muslims. In my heart, you're one nation, the only nation I belong to! Goodbye, and hopefully, we'll meet again soon! Yes, I'm leaving. The further I go in the range, the deeper I go into my Arab, Syrian, and Qalamouni belongings. Humanity can only be achieved in privacy.

Christ taught me to forgive. If God isn't the one who forgives in our hearts, how can we forgive our brothers in humanity for what is intolerable to distort it? May Allah throw forgiveness in my heart, for I am asking all of you to forgive any deficiency or error I have made. The prophets taught us to be thankful. There are many, many blessings I thank God Almighty for these thirty years in Qalamoun. "If you are thankful, I shall certainly increase (my blessings on) you."

My belief in reconciliation pushed me to create dialogue platforms among all the Syrian parties to consolidate the culture of coexistence and brotherhood. One day, I went on a mission to bridge the gap between the brothers in Northern Syria. It was a dangerous mission for I wanted to go on my own, with no accompanies. I told my loved ones to count me as dead in case I didn't return within three days.

My love for Syria was too great for me to imagine the disasters that befell it. It was also greater than the dreams of those who would like to cut it apart and take a piece of it for every sect. For me, Syria is this endless intermingling.

I never expected that the culture that I believed in would be the cause of my disappearance and my disappointment for not appreciating how great it is. A close-minded culture drew my end as Al-Hallaj said:

"My Host, with His ruthless courtesy,
Passed me His cup and bade me drink. I drank.
Round went with wine; sudden I heard Him cry:
Headsman! The Mat and the sword!"

Will I be able to return, like the awaited absentee? Nobody
knows … Forgive me.

A Secret Mission

Voices rose throughout the camp's yard. Refugees gathered from all around. The camp's women approached this gathering while carrying pots and pans. They were banging on them with large spoons to make a noise to draw the attention of camp administrators.

The officer, the camp administrator, shouted. "What is this noise? What happened? Why are you banging on the pots?"

The aide answered. "It's a protest … It seems like one, sir!"

The officer replied with astonishment. "A protest! Here at the camp! The weird thing about these Syrians! Whenever three of them gather, they name it a protest! As if they were out of the bottle, even the women started to demonstrate. And, anyway, what is this protest for? Did we miss any services? We offer food, drink, a tent for every family, doctors, school, clothes, etc … What is this ingratitude!"

Demonstrating women gathered around the officer in charge of managing the camp. They were protesting and denouncing such an administration and not seeking their requests. The shocked officer didn't understand what was going on around him and tried to calm the protesters. He didn't succeed anyway. The only thing left to do was to shout. And so, he did in his loud voice, asking them to be quiet, threatening once and again until calm was restored.

After the crowd fell silent, the officer said. "You ladies must form a committee to submit your requests. And if you don't do that, I won't listen to you. You must learn to be well-organized. Screaming and talking to everyone at the same time will not help you with anything."

The women retreated from the official and gathered around the oldest of them, Umm Mahmoud, to discuss what the officer had explained.

The women looked at her, trying to figure out what next step they would take. Umm Mahmoud calmed them down and said. "My friends, I heard what the officer said. We must not waste time, so let's directly form a committee consisting of five or six women. Let's also agree on what we will ask of him." Umm Mahmoud continued, saying, "We must first select the members of the committee. Whoever wants to nominate herself or another woman to be among the committee members, c'mon!"

The women were silent for a moment. They then began to consult among themselves and after a short period of deliberations and discussions to select suitable women to be among the committee members, they agreed to nominate Umm Mahmoud unanimously as the spokesperson for everyone.

Umm Mahmoud, known for her calm and wisdom, is a reference for everyone who has a problem in the camp. She's able to accommodate those around her with her patience and endurance. She sympathizes with their problems and helps them solve them. Therefore, she is the best representative of the protesters, especially since she was working as a lawyer in Syria. That is, she's aware of how to raise disputed issues. She had an office in Idlib until she became the target of attempted murder for her defense of detainees and detention centers. She was then smuggled by her sons to Turkey to save her life. For this reason, she uses the code name 'Umm Mahmoud' so that no one recognizes her.

The women continued to select the committee members, by choosing the most educated and the most present among them. They are Thanaa, the engineer, Heba, the teacher, Razan, the journalist, Rawan, the farmer, and Alia, the visual artist, and the number was completed.

Umm Mahmoud refused to be the only spokeswoman for the group, and she believed that the committee should share roles and ideas. She suggested that each of them should present a part of their requests in one clear and useful sentence so that the picture of the demands would be completed after each of them said what she had. As a result, their demands are clear to the officer. She added that they should make use of the time that will be allocated to them, and therefore they should not prolong the conversation so that they can persuade him, and he can respond to their requests.

Umm Mahmoud added. "We all know what we want. It's a single request, which is to obtain foodstuffs intended for the camp as raw materials and not as meals, as we currently get."

The women shook their heads in agreement, then she continued. "Here we have to agree on the method of presenting our request and the role of each of us in adding our requests to reach our goal, and I think that we have to start as follows:

- Thank the camp director and the host country for all the services that were provided to us and are still being provided.
- Show them how we cook and the spices we use in our countries, which differ somewhat from those used in Turkish cuisine.
- Praise the quantities of food provided to the camp residents.
- Explain that people's disliking the taste of food different from what they are accustomed to leads them to reject large quantities of it and thus waste it.
- Hope to give us the foodstuffs to cook by ourselves in the Syrian way and distribute them to the camp residents.
- The final requirement is to allow the use of the kitchen and its tools."

The women praised Umm Mahmoud's suggestion, distributed the roles, and agreed on the way to speak to the camp manager, making sure the sentences are clear, short, and straight to the point.

The women entered the camp manager's office headed by Umm Mahmoud and sat after the director welcomed them. As they agreed, Umm Mahmoud began and thanked the director for the great services he provides to the people of the camp. She also thanked the host country that prepared them and the camp residents in the camp to live safely and enjoy the conditions of elementary life as a person. These conditions were available even in their mother country. She then presented the participants in the delegation and introduced them, ending her speech by inviting them to present the problem in front of the director.

Thana said. "Turkish cooking is irreproachable, and it is one of the best eastern kitchens. No two can disagree on that. However, the spices used to add a special flavor to food, which is completely different from what the Syrians use in their food."

So Razan added. "There is no doubt that the quantities of food provided are sufficient, and sometimes more than sufficient. We cannot complain or even claim that no one has received an adequate amount of the food ration they are receiving."

"I would like to draw your attention, Mr. Officer, that the spices used by the Syrians are different from the spices used in Turkish food, which gives the food a flavor other than that which the Syrians are accustomed to. As a result, they leave the dishes full of what is left in them. Thus the percentage of food waste is at its highest, which leads to a great loss of morals and material," Hiba continued.

Alia followed up. "So after all we mentioned, we hope that you will accept the provision of raw food items for us so that we can cook them ourselves and distribute the cooked rations to the camp residents."

Rawan concluded by saying. "We also wish you to help us to get into the kitchen. We, in return, are going to divide ourselves into work groups. We will present to you lists in which we define the team that performs the work weekly. We will also clean used utensils and the kitchen so that we work to preserve public health in the camp."

The camp manager wrote down the women's requests and promised them that he would submit them to the

District Commissioner to make the final decision, and added. "If God wills, I'll come with the final answer within a week."

The women walked out of the camp manager's office, wonder clear in their eyes, as well as high hopes that their demands would be fulfilled. The women of the camp gathered around the delegation and heard what had been done and the camp manager's promise to raise their demands to the District Commissioner and promised to do his best to obtain the approval of the relevant authorities. The voices of the women prayed to the camp manager and God Almighty so that their requests would be seen with mercy.

Only three days later, the director had asked the committee who had met with him to come to his office. The women entered, accompanied by everyone's prayers for success. The camp residents hoped that they would bring back good news.

The camp manager said in a calm voice. "Congratulations ladies. What you wanted has happened and from next week you will receive the raw materials. You'll work on cooking and distributing them in the way you see is suitable. But everything must be organized and written. And for this, I hold Mrs. Umm Mahmoud responsible. I expect her attendance to provide me with lists of workers, materials, and those who receive food rations every week."

The ladies rejoiced, thanked the camp manager, and went away quietly. The women of the camp gathered in the yard far from the camp manager's office and began to congratulate one another for achieving what they wanted.

Umm Mahmoud said. "My friends, to succeed in what we seek, we must organize ourselves and divide the work among us, receiving materials and putting them in the store, for cooking, distributing meals, cleaning, and organizing lists of each committee. This is in addition to our undeclared mission, which is to transport food to the other side of the border in Syria daily, and this way requires choosing those who have the physical strength to carry and transport food, as the distance between us and the nearest village – as you know – exceeds ten kilometers. In addition, these women must display secrecy, determination, and strength."

She continued. "As everyone knows, we did all this to help our youth. Our young men remained in our villages to defend them, and they were suffering from a scarcity of foodstuff. Some of them eat once a day if they were lucky enough. As you notice my ladies, our youth have lost their bodies and can no longer continue their path, for one meal a day is not sufficient to provide them with energy and strength."

Umm Mahmoud finished off by saying. "So, my friends, our mission is difficult and dangerous. It requires us to be responsible enough to bear on our shoulders. Working silently and without drawing attention to what we do is of utmost importance. The issue for us is a matter of existence. Also, and most importantly, we must reduce our food rations, be content with little, and prevent the waste of any piece of bread because our youth need what we reduce from our meals."

A Message from the Security Branch

The jailer entered and called out. "AmalZahr El Dine. Released."

My feet did not help me to stand up, and I could not believe what I heard .. Released.

Released.

My cellmates repeated the word several times. I was completely distraught, for I fell into despair at the advent of this day that I had always dreamed of. Hope was far-fetched, especially after staying for a long time in the basement of the security branches and moving from one to another.

My cellmates released shouts of joy. They began to kiss me and kiss each other, finally, one of us got released and she'll go out again into the space of freedom. She will see the sky, the sun, and the moon. She will feel the wind and rain. One of us is meant to live again. One of us will come out of this grave.

The head of the cell said. "My daughter, once outside, scream at the top of your lungs. A scream for a thousand screams. A scream for us all that shakes the earth and the sky. A scream that summarizes our pain. A scream that shakes the mountains. A scream powerful enough to make the world's birds escape. A scream that reaches all ears. A scream that takes you to a free world, far away from our world."

Memories of the day I was arrested came back to my mind. I was fifteen years old that day. It was almost a year ago, but a year equivalent to fifty years. On that day, the security forces raided our house looking for my brother. Dozens of heavily armed men broke down the door of the house. We gathered behind my father, who extended out his hands to shield my mother, three brothers, and me (the eldest).

My father tried to calm down those who barged into our house, but their question was clear. "Where is your son?"

My father responded by saying that he did not know. "My son left the house when the events began. We know nothing about him."

One of them replied. "Don't you know anything about him? If you insist on that, then okay, you'll see." One of them pulled him out, knocked him to the ground and the beating began. More than ten people took turns hitting and kicking him with shoes and rifle butts. My father couldn't bear it, and he died.

Then the security men turned to my mother, who was trying with all her strength to close our eyes and shut our ears so that we wouldn't see what happened to my father. She was confident that her son wouldn't survive. One of them attacked her, screaming. "Are you going to speak, or do you also need someone to refresh your memory, as with your husband? Or do you want to follow him?"

My mother swore, confirming that she didn't know the whereabouts of my brother. However, she couldn't convince them. She was beaten and insulted. When they failed to obtain any information from her, the officer ordered his soldiers. "Take the girl. She'll remain with us in the security branch until her brother comes."

My mother cried out, pleading. "Please Mr. Officer. My daughter is still a child, she's not fifteen yet. I beg you. Have you not got any sisters or daughters? Have mercy on her." But it all was no use. A man whose feelings are diminished. He's as hard as a rock, the whole world means nothing to him.

I was pulled by my hand and herded like a sheep to their car, while my mother tried to reach me amid the cries of my brothers. It did not work.

The officer shouted in her face. "You only have two days. If your son comes and surrenders himself, we will let her go. If he's late, I do not guarantee you the fate of your child, especially with what she has in terms of scope. You know what she may be exposed to in the security branches. I hope that the importance of what I say is clear."

The security cars looted the road until we reached a cellar. They dragged me into the branch and dumped me in one of the cells. Women in the cell gathered around me and tried to touch me, but I was like a terrified bird. I screamed and shrank into a corner of the cell. So they left me to calm down.

One of them brought a glass of water and another brought a piece of bread. They asked me about my problem, so I told them the story of my brother and how I'm being held hostage until my brother surrendered himself within a maximum period of two days.

My cellmates exchanged looks, looks that were full of sadness. I assumed that it was sadness about what had happened to me. Little did I know it was sadness because of what was going to happen to me.

The first day passed and the second is about to end. My heart is racing faster for fear of what will come. Before the end of the specified period, my brother surrendered himself to the security branch. He sacrificed himself to save me. Unfortunately, this didn't happen. After he surrendered, his torment began. He had to acknowledge everything he had done. He had also to give the names of his colleagues who participated with him in the demonstrations and in writing on the walls.

He was beaten, insulted, electrocuted, and had his nails pulled out. Yet, they got no information from him. The security men were tired, and they brought the matter to the duty officer, who in turn looked at my brother's file. After seeing it, he said to his men. "There is one way to make him speak. Bring his sister to the investigation room."

I was pushed into the dark room and saw my brother, handcuffed, with blood on him. I cried and couldn't make any sound because of my fear. My brother shouted in tears. "My sister, no. I beg you, not my sister."

The officer said. "I conclude that you're now ready to confess everything? All we want is the names of the participants and the name of those leading you."

My brother said. "I don't know the names of the participants in the demonstrations. There was no one leading us, we just spontaneously set out and went to the street."

The officer yelled. "Spontaneously, you bastard? Spontaneously? How smart? As long as you want to play, let's play. I will ask you several questions. With every unanswered question, we take off a piece of your sister's clothes."

My brother cried out. "Oh God, where is your justice?"

The officer replied. "Cry out to God, to see if he'll help you!" He added. "The first question. Who is arranging your demonstrations?"

My brother cried, more like wailed and said. "There's no one. We were demonstrating spontaneously."

The officer said. "Wrong. Your answer is wrong." He turned to the guard and told him to take off my shirt, and so he did. "The second question. Which of your friends participated in the last demonstration?"

My brother shook his head and said. "The protestors were from all over the city. I didn't notice if one of my friends participated in the demonstration!"

The officer said. "For the second time, your answer is wrong. Guard, take off her pants."

I tried to resist, but the result was that my pants were taken off.

This torment lasted for many days. My brother and I were subjected to all kinds and methods of torture that no one could imagine. My brother uttered no word. Both our dignities were humiliated, until God answered his prayers and took out the spirit, he deposited on him.

The voice of the cell chief brought me back to reality as she said. "Oh, my daughter, today, you must try to forget the suffering that you endured. Think of your future far from this place and try with all your energy not to return to it." She then added. "But at the same time, do not forget that you have to carry our message to the world. It is a duty that we, the prisoners, whom you met in the security branches that you passed by during your detention period, trust you with. Be our tongue, speak in our name.

"And our message says, we detainees, prisoners, absentees from the world and present in the security branches, cry out to you and your consciences by asking, "Where are you, men of the country?

"Where are you from what is practiced against us in detention centers, we inform you, if you don't know, that we are here underground and in various places in the country. Where are you again, men of honor?

"Where are you men of dignity?

"How can you enjoy your freedom, while we are in torture centers? How can you sleep, while your eyes are never down? Our torments and constant pain have ended our sense of the alternation of night and day.

"Where are you men of the country who used our bodies as squares for your revenge?

"Our torturers are making us cry for your help, to come to our aid …

"They are mocking us because they know – and are certain – that you will not respond to us.

"They're certain that you won't heed the call.

"They continue with the series of rape. We're forced to completely get nude in front of these killers. We're presented in front of them as slaves. Everyone touches our body's private parts. They force us to say and do what we don't want to. We used to say and do what they want. We still do, perhaps they forgive us and relieve our suffering. We obey them and still do, perhaps our obedience makes us one of their concubines. As a result, we can have some extra food, hours of sleep, or a piece of soap.

"They mock you and your manhood, while they know that you won't come to our victory. We won't be released. We will remain in this darkness that tears a soul up. All that is humane in us got killed, the only thing left is our soul.

"So we, the dead-living prisoners or, as those in our case are called the living martyrs, ask you to destroy all the prisons and security branches on our heads and the heads of our torturers. Yes, destroy them with all your weapons, with all your power. Maybe, just maybe, by doing this, you'll wipe out your shame, as well as ours. Yes, destroy these places on us and everyone else, that's the least you could do.

"As for your claim that you got no missiles to destroy these branches, it is pathetic. For example, you possess missiles to fight among yourselves. You own them to achieve gains on the ground. You own them to destroy what remains of people, animals, and stones. You own them to consolidate your positions. You also own them to increase your authority over those around you ...!

"Alas, every one of you carries within him a little dictator ... this dictator who is waiting for an opportunity ... only one opportunity to rise to the surface and make his case.

Finally, we ask, "What is the meaning of the fight you claim? And what is the meaning of your battle when our honor is getting violated every moment!" She patted my shoulder. "This is our message, Godspeed. Good luck."

LOVE WITHIN DEFEAT

"Please sit down, gentlemen." This is how the Official Secretary of Homs began his speech with the security officers and officials there. He continued. "Today, gentlemen, we are going through the most difficult times that plague us and threaten our existence. Who would have expected that people with gentle morals and obedience, like the people of Homs, those famous for their humor and smiles, can be that violent? Moreover, they call what they do a 'revolution'!

"Unfortunately, I can now say we're almost losing control of the city. All this prompted me to call for this emergency meeting to ward off the consequences of this disobedience and to lay down a plan to stop this deteriorating security, especially since this movement began to attract young men and women from Homs, as well as its elderlies. They made Homs a symbol of revolution. Some of them even called it the revolution's capital. Therefore, we had to make a move quickly and cautiously to restore calm in it at any cost, even if we had to work on separating its people. I think that it is very easy, as the people of this city to belong to many sects, which will make our mission possibly successful. I'm waiting for your views and suggestions. Please ..."

Dean Ahmed said. "Sir, after witnessing the recent demonstrations and events, we no longer notice fear in the eyes of people. Their leaders have even dared to announce themselves, so I suggest that we carry out a raid campaign throughout the city and arrest the activists in it, the owners of the so-called civil movement."

The Official Secretary shook his head and gave the word to Dean Zuhri, who said. "I think that our first task is to prevent the demonstrators from reaching the main city square, as we don't want them to stage a sit-in and imitate Egyptian youth in Tahrir Square. So, I suggest that we do so by covering the entire square with broken glass to prevent the demonstrators from entering. Whoever dares to enter, we kill them."

The Official Secretary replied. "Beautiful, beautiful. But, until now, I have not heard any suggestion that fits what I presented to you. The question remains: 'How will we be able to cultivate division among the people of the city?'"

Moments of silence were broken by Dean Majeed, who said. "I've got a suggestion, the least we can describe it with is dangerous. Gentlemen, we all know that the honor of the family is everyone's priority. Therefore, if a group of girls from Homs were abducted and assaulted, we'll create great confusion … especially if these women belong to one sect and we accuse another sect of this act. At the same time, we throw weapons in their hands so that they will use them against one another. Later, we intervene and eliminate the rest of the rebels among them. What do you think?"

The Official Secretary liked this idea, which he described as hellish. "We'll implement all your requests. And most importantly, the last one, which must be our primary goal, not because it will achieve our goal of spreading the spirit of division among the people of the city, but also because it will make them fall into the bump and get armed. This will justify our use of violence against them. And then, what was said by one of the leaders of their popular movement, Abdul Aziz Al-Khair, in his warning to them that 'if the revolution becomes armed, it becomes Muslim ... and if it becomes Muslim, it will be sectored' will come true."

The clock ticked and the security began to implement the plan that was set. The first goal was to intercept and kidnap a bus transporting girls from a Sunni neighborhood to the university. The girls were secretly driven to an underground security branch. The security personnel were surprised by the visitors to the branch, but none of them would dare to ask for the reason behind this.

The fifty frightened girls were crammed into one cell. An hour later, the ritual torture began. The first ritual was aimed at breaking their dignity, by issuing the first order for them to take off their clothes completely, even their underwear. But some of the girls objected and refused. As a result, they were subjected to all kinds of violence, such as slapping and kicking, etc ... They were then forced to stand together in front of the officers and recruiters.

The girls stood shyly, each placing their hands on a part of her body, trying to cover it while quietly crying.

The head of the security branch ordered the branch's personnel and officers to pass in front of the ladies. They were told to look at them the way he used to do with women in slave markets, to inspect them like goods. He was harsh with every member who tried to evade looking them in the face.

Hassan was one of the personnel. He was a young man in his twenties belonging to the Alawite sect. He couldn't stand straight, and he trembled due shocked by the horrific scene. So, the branch chief's loud voice surprised him, and he slowly passed in front of every girl standing in line to look at them.

Hassan started walking with his eyes closed, trying to save these ladies from embarrassment, for he saw his mother and sisters in them. The branch chief noticed him and forced him to open his eyes saying, "Open your eyes, Hassan. Don't you dare do that again, otherwise your punishment will be severe?"

Hesitating, Hassan opened his eyes and they fell on a block of light. She was a girl who shined a bright white. It was the type of white, in which its radiance cannot be accommodated in the place where it is confined. She had long, deep black hair, falling on her breasts as if to hide and protect them. Her arms fell by her body's sides, and her hands were so soft, with long fingers like those of an artist. The girl tried to hide her nakedness using her hands. As for her legs, they were clasped together and her feet, like a pair of pigeons, were tapped by the ground to protect her from its cold.

Hassan stood still, as he contemplated what God had created. He wondered. 'Is it possible for such beauty to exist in this world?'

The girl looked up at him with fear and shame. He saw her gorgeous black eyes, like black olives. In her gaze, he saw her pleading with him to stop looking at her. He lowered his eyes in shame. Hassan saw all women of the world in this girl. She's become closer to him than the sky. He fell for her, and she fell for him. He became her destiny, as she became his destiny. The throne of love over her body covered her with jasmine. Love, at first sight, swept them off their feet like a flood. They flew into a world far from their surroundings. He whispered to her when she returned to her cell. "Don't be afraid. I won't leave you. We'll escape together. Just bear with me a little."

It was decided to transfer the prisoners to another branch, the location of which is known only to a small number of people. Here came the opportunity Hassan had been waiting for and he arranged the escape by bribing the guards and the truck driver.

The girls got into the prison's truck, including Hassan's love, Amar. In the middle of the road, the truck stopped and opened its door. Hassan called Amar, who jumped out quickly accompanied by the prayers of the women. They then disappeared.

Later, they were in Turkey. And they announced their marriage. Together, they lived a love story that surpassed all differences and barriers.

Marie Thérèse Kiriaky

- Is a Syrian author, journalist, and feminist activist. She was born in Damascus, Syria.
- Is the founding member and the President of the Arab Austrian Women, in Vienna, Austria. Kiriaky is also the Headmistress and a teacher at the Arabic Language School of the Association.
- Is the founder and director of the *Balsam* project, which does charitable work to the benefit of Syrian refugee children and women.
- Is the editor-in-chief of *Balsam* magazine, published by the Arab Austrian Women, based in Vienna, Austria.
- Is a member of the governing body of the Arab Human Rights Organization, Austria branch.
- Is a co-founder of the Syrian Women's Political Movement.
- Has worked at the United Nations from 1987 to 2015 (UNRWA and then the United Nations Office on Drugs and Crime).
- Is the founding member of the United Nations Arab Staff Association, in Vienna, Austria.
- In 2015 she won the United Nations Secretary General Award for voluntarism on her project *Balsam*.
- In 2016 she won the sponsorship of the United Nations Women's Guild – Vienna/Austria for her project *Balsam*.
- In 2017 she won the sponsorship of the United Nations Women's Guild – New York/USA for her project *Balsam*.
- Is a contributor to social work in Damascus, Syria by setting-up literacy classes for four years, in addition to her activities supporting women.

- She writes articles related to women and human rights and publishes her articles on multiple electronic pages.
- Has obtained a BA degree in the French Literature from the Faculty of Arts, Damascus University in 1984.
- Has studied elementary school in Jesuit schools in Hama (the interior section) and finished her preparatory and secondary studies in El-Mahabbah and Seventh Schools in Damascus.

- Grauzone: Kurzgeschichten-Dar Alhadarah- Cairo 2014 in Arabic language, Club Pen, Austria in German language.
- Escaping Forward (Stories)- Dar Alhadarah- Cairo 2015.

Translated by: Ms. Wedyan Mortada
Edited by: Ms. Susan Cohen-Ugar

HERZ FÜR AUTOREN A HEART FOR AUTHORS À L'ÉCOUTE DES AUTEURS MIA KAP
FÖR FÖRFATTARE UN CORAZÓN POR LOS AUTORES YAZARLARIMIZA GÖNÜL
PER AUTORI ET HJERTE FOR FORFATTERE EEN HART VOOR SCHRIJVERS TE
INKÉRT SERCE DLA AUTORÓW EIN HERZ FÜR AUTOREN A HEART FOR AUTH
ВСЕЙ ДУШОЙ К АВТОРАМ ETT HJÄRTA FÖR FÖRFATTARE A LA ESCUCHA
MIA ΚΑΡΔΙΑ ΓΙΑ ΣΥΓΓΡΑΦΕΙΣ UN CUORE PER AUTORI ET HJERTE FOR FORF
RZÓINKÉRT SERCE DLA AUTORÓW
RAÇÃO ВСЕЙ ДУШОЙ К АВТОРАМ ET

The author

Marie Thérèse Kiriaky is a Syrian author,
journalist and feminist activist. She worked at
the United Nations for almost three decades. Ms
Kiriaky completed her studies in Syria, including
a Bachelor's in French Literature from the
Damascus University. Human rights, in particular
women's rights are close to her heart as she has
written many articles on these topics. Ms Kiriaky
has published two books, this being the English
version of Escaping Forward (Stories) from 2015.

Ms Kiriaky is the Founder and President of the
Arab Austrian Women's Association, as well as
the Co-Founder of the Syrian Women's Political
Movement. In 2015 she won the United Nations
Secretary General Award for Voluntarism for her
Project Balsam. The United Nations Women's
Guild in Vienna and New York chose to award
their annual sponsorship among many other
candidates to Project Balsam in 2016 and 2017
as well.